Janet Hayward has over 15 years' experience in the beauty industry and is the co-founder of the beauty and health website, beautydirectory.com.au, which is followed by beauty experts worldwide. Originally from the United Kingdom, Janet now lives in Sydney, Australia with her family.

Aimee Twigger is a young baker, crafter and blogger from Devon, England. On her blog Twigg Studios Aimee shares recipes with thousands of readers across the US, UK, and Europe. She is the author of *Love Aimee, X* published in 2015 and its companion *Aimee's Perfect Bakes*.

Arielle Gamble is a talented illustrator and designer, based in New South Wales, Australia. Arielle loves to work with ink and watercolours, and much of her work explores themes around the natural world

First published in Great Britain in 2016 by Modern Books
An imprint of Elwin Street Productions Limited
3 Percy Street
London W1T 1DE
www.elwinstreet.com

ISBN 978-1-906761-77-6
10 9 8 7 6 5 4 3 2 1

Printed in China

TEATIME
TREATS

Janet Hayward &
Aimee Twigger

with illustrations by
Arielle Gamble

(m)

CONTENTS

INTRODUCTION

Mass-produced food can never compete with the taste of treats made with the love and care of your own hands. There is such pleasure to be found in baking a cake or other treat from scratch. Bringing together simple ingredients that, through an almost alchemical process, become delicious desserts, cakes, biscuits and sweets.

Whether you are looking for teatime treats to share with friends or delectable gifts to indulge the family, you will find the perfect recipe in this book. Alongside traditional favourites we have included recipes for vegan cupcakes (p. 10) and fudge (p. 81), as well as a gluten-free chocolate cake (p. 14), so you can cater to all tastes and needs.

These fun and straightforward recipes will suit all experience levels; all the ingredients are readily available from most high-street stores and no fancy or complicated techniques are called for. Tips and recommendations of alternative flavourings are dotted throughout to help you make the most of each recipe.

So stock up the pantry and let's get baking!

These recipes are a classic assortment of delicious cakes and bakes, all which are simple to make and delicious to eat. Here you'll find a wealth of traditional recipes alongside some modern twists on old favourites. Includes cakes for special occasions and quiet Sunday-afternoon baking projects for sharing, or keeping to yourself.

Apple and Fig Millefeuilles

Red Velvet Cupcakes

Lemon Drizzle Cake

Rich Amaranth Chocolate Cake

Egg-free Carrot Cake

Apple and Almond Cake

Classic New York Cheesecake

Spiced Gingerbread

Coconut Cake

Classic French Lemon Tart

Victoria Sponge

Grandma's Apple Pie

Rich Fruitcake

CLASSIC CAKES & BAKES

APPLE AND FIG MILLEFEUILLES

MAKES 6

1 lemon
5 cooking apples, peeled cored and chopped
225 g dried figs, chopped
250 ml apple cider
60 g caster sugar
1 teaspoon ground cinnamon,
  plus extra to serve
4 sheets of filo pastry
flour, for dusting
3 teaspoons icing sugar
vegetable oil, for brushing

Preheat the oven to 200°C. Line a baking sheet with baking paper.

Peel the rind from the lemon in wide strips. Squeeze half the lemon. In a 3-litre saucepan, mix together the lemon rind and juice, the apples, figs, apple cider, caster sugar and cinnamon. Cover and bring to the boil, then lower the heat and simmer, for 10 minutes, until the apples are just tender. Remove from the heat and leave to cool.

Separate one sheet of the filo pastry and lay it on a floured board. Brush it lightly with vegetable oil and lay another sheet on top. Repeat to make a stack of four sheets of pastry. Using a sharp knife, carefully cut the stack of pastry sheets lengthways into three equal strips. Then cut each strip into six equal rectangles.

Transfer the pastry stacks onto the prepared baking sheet and bake for up to 8 minutes, until crisp and golden. Remove from the oven and transfer to a wire rack.

Assemble the millefeuilles immediately before serving. Place one pastry piece on a serving plate and top with the apple and fig mixture. Place a second pastry piece on top of that and add more of the fruit. Top with a third pastry piece and sprinkle with icing sugar and a little more cinnamon. Repeat with the remaining fruit mixture and pastry pieces until you have six millefeuille towers.

RED VELVET CUPCAKES

The beetroot gives these cupcakes an attractive deep-red colour and makes for a moist bake. The base recipe is vegan and you can spruce it up by topping each cupcake with extravagant icing.

MAKES 12

225 g cooked beetroot
100 ml rapeseed oil
juice of 1 lemon
1 teaspoon vanilla essence
175 g plain flour
200 g granulated sugar
3 tablespoons cocoa powder
1 teaspoon baking powder

Preheat the oven to 190°C. Grease a 12-hole cupcake tin or line with paper cases.

Place the beetroot in a food processor with the rapeseed oil, lemon juice, vanilla essence and 60 ml of cold water. Blend to a smooth purée.

Place the flour in a large bowl and mix together with the sugar, cocoa powder and baking powder.

Add the wet ingredients to the dry ingredients and mix to combine. Spoon the mixture into the cupcake tin and bake for 20 minutes, until risen and cooked through. Leave the cupcakes to cool before decorating with your choice of icing.

LEMON DRIZZLE CAKE

SERVES 6

120 ml light olive oil, plus extra
for greasing
200 g self-raising flour
50 g ground almonds
150 g caster sugar, plus
100 g for the glaze
pinch of salt
4 tablespoons milk
1 large egg
grated zest and juice of 1 large lemon

Preheat the oven to 180°C. Grease a ring cake tin measuring approximately 18 x 13 cm and base-line with baking paper.

Combine the dry ingredients in a large bowl. In a blender whizz together the oil, milk, egg and lemon zest. Fold the liquid quickly into the dry ingredients. Turn the batter into the prepared cake tin and bake for about 50 minutes. The cake is ready when a skewer inserted into the centre comes out clean.

While the cake is baking, mix the lemon juice and sugar for the glaze, stirring from time to time, until the sugar dissolves. Pour the glaze over the hot cake while still in its tin. Allow the cake to cool in the tin, but turn it out before it goes completely cold. Peel off the baking paper.

RICH AMARANTH CHOCOLATE CAKE

This is a delicious cake with the perfect combination of earthy, fudgy and comfortably chocolatey elements. Amaranth flour is gluten-free, but this recipe also works well with spelt, wheat or quinoa flour.

SERVES 8

200 g unsalted butter, softened, plus extra
  for greasing
200 g dark chocolate, roughly chopped
1 tablespoon agave syrup
6 large eggs
1 teaspoon vanilla essence
1 teaspoon sea salt flakes
250 g amaranth flour

Preheat the oven to 180°C. Grease a deep, 20-cm round cake tin and line with baking paper.

Melt the butter with the chocolate in a medium bowl over a saucepan of simmering water or in the microwave. In a large bowl, combine the agave syrup and eggs. Beat until the mixture is fluffy and has doubled in volume. Beat in the vanilla and salt. Stir in the chocolate mixture. Sift in the amaranth flour and stir to combine well.

Pour the batter into the prepared cake tin. Bake for 40 to 45 minutes, until the cake is set and jiggles only slightly when the tin is gently shaken. Allow the cake to cool in the tin, but remove it before it goes completely cold. Peel off the baking paper and allow the cake to cool completely before slicing.

EGG-FREE CARROT CAKE

The secret to success lies in the long, slow baking of this cake – keep the oven temperature low and be patient! Carrot decorations can often be found in the home-baking section of a supermarket or in specialist cookery shops.

SERVES 4

115 g unsalted butter, plus extra
 for greasing
225 g self-raising flour
1 tablespoon ground cinnamon
1 teaspoon ground nutmeg
115 ml honey
115 g caster sugar
225 g carrots, peeled and grated
icing sugar, for dusting

Preheat the oven to 170˚C. Grease a 20-cm spring-form cake tin and base-line with baking paper.

Sift the flour and spices together into a large mixing bowl. Melt the butter in a small saucepan over a low heat, add the honey and sugar, and stir until the sugar has dissolved. Pour the sugar and butter mixture into the spiced flour, add the carrots and mix well. Spoon the mixture into the prepared cake tin and bake for 75 minutes until a skewer inserted into the centre of the cake comes out clean.

Allow the cake to cool in the tin for 10 minutes before turning it out. Peel off the baking paper, dust with icing sugar and decorate with tiny carrot decorations, if available.

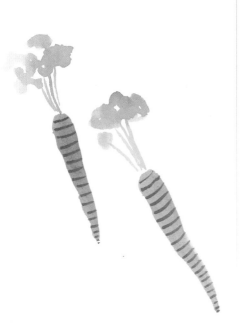

APPLE AND ALMOND CAKE

This recipe uses the classic combination of apple, almond and cinnamon to make a moist, warmly spiced cake with a light texture. Decorate with flaked almonds and serve warm with whipped cream or Greek yogurt to make this cake extra special.

SERVES 6

175 g unsalted butter, softened,
  plus extra for greasing
2 tablespoons brown sugar
4 apples, peeled, cored and sliced
1 teaspoon ground cinnamon
125 g caster sugar
2 eggs, beaten
1 teaspoon almond essence
75 g self-raising flour
75 g ground almonds

Preheat the oven to 150°C. Grease a 20-cm spring-form cake tin and base-line with baking paper.

Melt 25 g of the butter in a frying pan, stir in the brown sugar and keep stirring until the mixture bubbles. Add the apples and cinnamon, and cook gently, turning occasionally, until the apples are tender and slightly caramelized. Remove from the heat.

In a large bowl, beat the remaining butter with the caster sugar, until light and fluffy. Gradually beat in the eggs and almond essence. Gently fold in the flour and ground almonds, and spoon the mixture into the prepared cake tin. Smooth the surface and arrange the cooked apple slices on top. Pour any juices left in the frying pan over the batter.

Bake for 45 minutes, using a skewer to check that it is cooked through. Leave the cake to cool in the tin for a few minutes before turning it out. Peel off the baking paper.

CLASSIC NEW YORK CHEESECAKE

This creamy cake is perfect served on its own or with your favourite choice of topping, berries work particularly well. To ensure a smooth consistency, bring the cream cheese to room temperature before using.

SERVES 4

150 g digestive biscuits, finely crushed
115 g unsalted butter, melted
700 g cream cheese
200 g caster sugar
2 teaspoons vanilla essence
4 eggs, beaten

for the topping
475 ml soured cream
2 tablespoons caster sugar
½ teaspoon vanilla essence

Preheat the oven to 180°C.

In a large bowl, mix the biscuit crumbs with the melted butter and press the mixture into the bottom of a 25-cm spring-form cake tin. Use the back of a spoon to smooth it out and press it firmly into place.

Mix the cream cheese with the sugar and vanilla essence, then gradually add the beaten eggs without over-beating the mixture.

Spoon the cream cheese mix into the cake tin, smooth the top and bake for 30 minutes.

To make the topping, mix the soured cream, sugar and vanilla essence together. Once the cheesecake has baked for 30 minutes, take it out of the oven, pour the topping over the cake and return the cheesecake to the oven for a further 10 minutes.

Leave the cheesecake to cool, then chill completely before removing it from the tin and serving.

SPICED GINGERBREAD

SERVES 8

225 g unsalted butter, plus extra
 for greasing
450 g plain flour
1½ teaspoons each of ground ginger,
 cinnamon and allspice
½ teaspoon ground cloves
¼ teaspoon salt
200 g chopped dates
100 g chopped walnuts
240 ml molasses
130 g dark brown sugar
4 large eggs, beaten
1 teaspoon bicarbonate of soda
1 tablespoon warm milk

Preheat the oven to 180°C. Grease a deep, 20-cm square cake tin and line with nonstick baking paper.

Sift the flour, spices and salt into a large bowl. Stir in the dates and nuts. Gently melt together the butter, molasses and sugar either in a medium bowl over a saucepan of simmering water or in the microwave. Add to the dry ingredients, together with the eggs and the baking soda mixed with the milk. Combine thoroughly.

Spoon the mixture into the prepared cake tin and bake for 20 minutes. Reduce the oven temperature to 150°C and bake for another hour, or until a skewer inserted into the centre comes out clean.

Cool the gingerbread in its tin before turning it out onto a wire rack. Peel off the baking paper and leave the gingerbread to cool completely. Serve in thick, generously buttered, slices.

COCONUT CAKE

This light and airy cake is a lovely addition to an afternoon tea or add berries and coconut flaked icing for a special occasion. Rose water is an amazingly versatile ingredient and is a handy item to have in the pantry.

SERVES 8

200 g creamed coconut, grated
45 ml rapeseed oil
200 g cream cheese
200 g granulated sugar
45 ml rosewater
1 teaspoon vanilla essence
6 eggs, beaten
375 g plain flour
2 tablespoons ground almonds
200 g desiccated coconut

Preheat the oven to 170°C. Grease a deep, 20-cm round cake tin and base-line with baking paper.

Melt the creamed coconut in a medium saucepan or in the microwave. Stir in the rapeseed oil and set aside to cool. In a large bowl, beat the cream cheese and sugar together, then mix in the creamed coconut and rapeseed oil mixture, the rosewater, vanilla essence and eggs. Beat the mixture until fluffy, then fold in the flour, ground almonds and desiccated coconut.

Spoon the mixture into the prepared cake tin and bake for approximately 1 hour until a skewer inserted into the centre comes out clean.

Turn the cake out onto a wire rack, peel off the baking paper and leave to cool before slicing.

CLASSIC FRENCH LEMON TART

SERVES 8

85 g unsalted butter, cubed,
  plus extra for greasing
175 g plain flour
1 tablespoon icing sugar
4 egg yolks
180 ml lemon juice
25 g cornflour
3 egg yolks
115 g caster sugar
150 ml double cream
grated zest of 1 lemon

To make the pastry, rub the butter into the flour using your fingertips. Stir in the icing sugar and one egg yolk and mix well. Gradually add cold water, a splash at a time, until the dough comes together and is soft but not sticky. Gather the dough into a ball, wrap it in a plastic food bag and chill for 20 minutes.

Preheat the oven to 190°C. Grease a 20- to 23-cm, fluted pie tin.

Roll the pastry out thinly and use it to line the pie tin. Prick the base and leave for 20 minutes. Now line the pastry with baking paper and fill with baking beans. Bake for 15 minutes, remove the beans and paper, and return to the oven for 5 more minutes. Set aside. Turn the oven down to 180°C.

To make the filling, add enough cold water to the lemon juice to make it up to 450 ml. Transfer to a small saucepan and beat in the cornflour. Turn on the heat and gradually bring the mixture to the boil, stirring constantly. When the consistency is like a thick sauce, take the saucepan off the heat and allow the mixture to cool.

Beat in the remaining egg yolks, caster sugar, cream and lemon zest, and return the saucepan to the heat. Gradually bring to the boil, stirring constantly. As soon as the mixture begins to bubble, pour it into the pastry case and bake for 20 minutes. Chill thoroughly before serving.

VICTORIA SPONGE

This classic, lightweight sandwich cake is a definite crowd-pleaser.
The sponge should be firm yet well aerated with a decadent layer of
raspberry jam. To make this cake even more luxurious spread whipped
double cream over the jam before sandwiching the two cakes.

SERVES 8

110 g unsalted butter, softened,
 plus extra for greasing
110 g caster sugar, plus one tablespoon
 for dusting
2 large eggs, beaten
¼ teaspoon vanilla essence
110 g self-raising flour
½ teaspoon baking powder
2 tablespoons milk or water (if needed)
2 tablespoons raspberry jam

Preheat the oven to 180°C. Grease two shallow, 18-cm round cake tins and base-line with baking paper.

In a large bowl, beat the butter and sugar together until pale and so light that the mixture drops from the spoon or whisk. Add the egg, a spoonful at a time, beating thoroughly between each addition. If the mixture curdles, add a spoonful of the flour and continue beating. Beat in the vanilla essence.

Sift together the flour and baking powder, and fold into the beaten mixture. The batter should be soft enough to drop from the spoon. If needed, add the milk or water to loosen it.

Divide the mixture evenly between the cake tins and bake for 25 to 30 minutes, until the sponges feel firm and springy in the centre. Cool on a wire rack and peel off the baking paper before sandwiching the two halves together with raspberry jam. Dust the top with caster sugar.

GRANDMA'S APPLE PIE

Warm apple pie is the perfect antidote to grey winter days and is delicious served with custard or vanilla ice cream. Any variety of cooking apples can be used but Bramley or Granny Smith apples work particularly well.

SERVES 8

225 g unsalted butter, softened
200 g golden caster sugar, plus extra
 for sprinkling
2 eggs
360 g plain flour, plus 3 tablespoons
1 kg cooking apples
pinch each of ground cinnamon,
 nutmeg and allspice

To make the pastry, beat the butter and 50 g of the sugar together until just mixed, then add one whole egg and the yolk from the second egg (saving the white). Beat the mixture until it starts to resemble scrambled egg – this should take about 1 minute. Add the flour, in three parts, stirring with a wooden spoon to combine. The mixture will begin to form a ball, so help it along with your hands, then wrap it in a plastic food bag and chill for 45 minutes.

While the dough chills, peel and core the apples, then chop them into bite-sized pieces and rest on kitchen paper to soak up any juices. Place the apple pieces in a large bowl with the remaining sugar, the 3 tablespoons of flour and the spices. Mix lightly with your fingers.

Preheat the oven to 190°C. Roll out two-thirds of the pastry to generously line a 20-cm pie tin.

Toss the apples into the pie tin. Brush the edge of the pastry with a little water to help create a seal. Roll out the rest of the pastry, lay it over the apples and pinch around the edges to seal. Trim off any excess pastry and make a few slits in the lid to let steam escape. Brush the top of the pie with the leftover egg white and sprinkle with sugar. Bake for 45 minutes until the pastry is golden.

RICH FRUITCAKE

SERVES 8

225 g unsalted butter, softened,
  plus extra for greasing
300 g caster sugar
4 large eggs, beaten
45 ml brandy
300 g plain flour
¼ teaspoon ground nutmeg
¼ teaspoon ground cinnamon
200 g each of currants, raisins
  and sultanas
70 g chopped almonds

Preheat the oven to 150°C. Grease a deep, 23-cm round cake tin and base-line with baking paper.

In a large bowl, beat the butter and sugar together until pale and fluffy. In a separate bowl, combine the eggs and brandy and mix well. Beat the egg into the butter and sugar mixture, a little at a time. Adding a spoonful of flour with the last few additions will prevent the mixture from curdling.

Sift the flour and spices into the bowl and fold them into the beaten mixture. Finally, fold in the dried fruit and nuts until evenly distributed.

Spoon the mixture into the prepared cake tin and bake for approximately 2 hours, or until a skewer inserted into the centre comes out clean.

Leave the cake to cool in its tin before turning it out and peeling off the baking paper.

Make and serve a delightfully traditional high tea for friends and family with these delicious recipes. You can jump straight to the cakes and biscuits for a simple tea for two, or explore the savoury recipes for a larger event. The delicate treats in this chapter are so good that you will want to make them again and again, and you'll always find yourself hoping it's time for tea.

HIGH TEA

CUCUMBER SANDWICHES

Perfect in their simplicity, cucumber sandwiches are a staple of an English high tea. Getting the seasoning right is key to the success of these delicate afternoon treats.

MAKES 9

½ cucumber, peeled
salt
6 thin slices of good-quality white bread
unsalted butter, softened
ground white pepper

Slice the cucumber as thinly as you can and layer the slices in a colander or sieve. Sprinkle lightly with salt and leave for 20 minutes, then pat the cucumber dry using kitchen paper.

Butter each slice of bread generously. Arrange cucumber slices on one slice of bread, overlapping each slice. Sprinkle with white pepper and top with a second slice of bread. Repeat with the remaining bread and cucumber. Pressing down firmly, cut the crusts off the three rounds of bread, then cut each into three neat fingers of roughly equal size. Serve immediately.

TOMATO AND PESTO TARTS

These tarts are perfect as a light lunch or as a delicious savoury addition to high tea. Make these tarts extra special by making your own pesto.

MAKES 8

flour, for dusting
320 g puff pastry, fresh or frozen
2 tablespoons pesto
12 ripe tomatoes, thinly sliced
1 egg yolk
2 tablespoons finely grated hard cheese
1 tablespoon extra virgin olive oil
8 sprigs of basil
salt
freshly ground black pepper

Preheat the oven to 200°C. Line two baking sheets with baking paper.

On a lightly floured board, roll out the pastry thinly. Cut out eight 12-cm discs and arrange them on the prepared baking sheets. Using a smaller cutter, lightly score a 1-cm border through the pastry.

Spread the centre of each pastry disc with a little pesto and arrange tomato slices in an overlapping spiral on top.

Mix the egg yolk with one teaspoon of cold water and glaze the tops of the pastry borders. (Take care not to brush the sides, as this will prevent the layers separating and the pastry rising.) Season the tarts with salt and pepper, sprinkle with the cheese and drizzle the olive oil over the tomatoes.

Bake for approximately 15 minutes, until well risen and golden. Top with a sprig of basil and serve warm.

CHEESE GOUGÈRES

Choux pastry is a French favourite. Classically, it is used to make sweet profiteroles, but it can be used in savoury dishes, too. These buns should be crisp and golden on the outside, and light and fluffy within. Serve them warm or cold as canapés.

SERVES 4

115 g butter
½ teaspoon salt
140 g plain flour
4 eggs, beaten
115 g cheddar cheese, grated

Preheat the oven to 220°C. Line a baking sheet with baking paper.

Place the butter and the salt in a saucepan with 250 ml of cold water. Bring to the boil, then reduce the heat to low and add the flour in a single batch. Stir rapidly and continuously with a wooden spoon as the mixture comes together. Cook for up to 3 minutes, until the mixture forms a smooth ball. Take the saucepan off the heat and leave it cool for a few minutes.

Add the beaten eggs to the warm dough, in four batches beating thoroughly after each to incorporate. Finally, stir in the grated cheese.

Put small spoonfuls of the mixture onto the prepared baking sheet, leaving room between each spoonful for the pastry to puff up.

Bake for 10 minutes, turn the heat down to 180°C and cook for a further 15 minutes, until the gougères are cooked through and golden.

BUCKWHEAT BLINIS WITH SALMON AND CREAM CHEESE

Make these traditional Russian canapés to accompany champagne for a celebration or as the highlight of an elegant high tea.

MAKES 12

125 ml milk
5 g fast-action dried yeast
1 egg, separated
75 g buckwheat or spelt flour
pinch of salt
vegetable oil, for frying
100 g cream cheese
150 g smoked salmon, cut into strips
handful of dill

Warm the milk gently until it is tepid and divide equally between two small bowls. Dissolve the yeast in one of the bowls of milk and leave it to stand for 45 minutes in a warm place – bubbles should appear on the surface.

Beat the egg yolk into the second bowl of milk and then transfer both mixtures to a large mixing bowl. Mix in the flour and salt, cover with a damp cloth and leave in a warm place for 1 hour. Beat the egg white until it forms stiff peaks and gently fold into the dough.

Lightly oil a large, heavy-based frying pan and allow it to heat before dropping small spoonfuls of the dough mixture onto the hot surface. Cook gently for up to 2 minutes on each side, until puffy and golden.

Spread a thin layer of cream cheese on each blini and top with smoked salmon and dill.

PERFECT SCONES

These scones are delicious served warm with salted butter or cool with clotted cream and strawberry jam. To keep your scones light and airy keep kneading to a minimum, just enough to combine the dough.

MAKES 12

75 g unsalted butter, cubed and softened,
  plus extra for greasing
225 g self-raising flour, plus extra
  for dusting
pinch of salt
3 tablespoons golden caster sugar
1 large egg, beaten
2 tablespoons buttermilk,
  plus extra for glazing
50 g raisins (optional)

Preheat the oven to 220°C. Grease a baking sheet.

Sift the flour and salt into a large mixing bowl, rub the butter into the flour mixture using your fingertips until it looks like breadcrumbs. Stir in the sugar. Combine the egg with the buttermilk, then add to the flour mixture in four parts, along with the raisins, if using. Stir the mix with a spatula as it binds together to form a dough.

When the mixture has become a ball, lift it out of the bowl and onto a floured surface. Use a rolling pin to lightly roll out the dough until it is 2.5 cm thick. Using a 5-cm pastry cutter, cut out as many scones as possible. Gather the scraps to roll out again and repeat.

Place the scones onto the prepared baking sheet and brush the tops with buttermilk. Bake for 10 to 12 minutes, until the scones have risen and are golden brown.

FAVOURITE CHOCOLATE BROWNIES

Everyone loves a chocolate brownie. Super simple to make, they should
be slightly gooey in the middle with a satisfying gentle resistance
when bitten into.

MAKES 16

200 g dark chocolate, broken into pieces
100 g unsalted butter, softened
250 g granulated sugar
4 large eggs, beaten
1 teaspoon vanilla essence
60 g plain flour
60 g cocoa powder

Preheat the oven to 180°C. Grease a deep, 20-cm square cake tin and base-line with baking paper.

Place the chocolate pieces in a bowl and melt over a saucepan of simmering water or in the microwave. Set aside to cool slightly. Place the butter and sugar in a large bowl, and beat with an electric mixer until light and fluffy, then gradually add the beaten eggs, mixing well after each addition.

Beat in the vanilla essence, then pour in the cooled, melted chocolate and mix thoroughly. Sift the flour and cocoa powder into the mixture and gently fold in using a metal spoon. When fully combined, spoon the mixture into the prepared cake tin and spread evenly.

Bake for 20 to 25 minutes until firm to the touch. The brownie should be soft in the middle, but the top should be cracked. Leave to cool for at least 20 minutes in the tin, then turn it out and peel off the baking paper. Place the brownie on a cutting board and cut into 5-cm squares.

IRRESISTIBLE SHORTBREAD

MAKES 34

225 g unsalted butter, softened
120 g caster sugar
280 g plain flour, plus extra for shaping
1 teaspoon salt
2 tablespoons vanilla sugar

Neatly line two baking sheets with baking paper.

In a large bowl, beat the butter and sugar together until pale and light. Sift the flour and salt into the bowl and work into the butter mix to form a soft dough. Chill for 30 minutes.

Take a piece of dough the size of a walnut and roll into a ball using the palms of your hands. Repeat until all the dough has been used and set the balls well apart on the baking sheets. Use the back of a fork dipped in flour to flatten each ball into a disc marked with the tines. Chill once more.

Preheat the oven to 140°C. Bake for 45 minutes, then turn the oven down to 110°C and bake for another hour to dry without taking any colour.

Dredge the biscuits with vanilla sugar while still hot from the oven and before transferring them to a wire rack to cool.

SERVING HIGH TEA

High tea is a great way to add a touch of elegance and occasion to an afternoon gathering. The following is a selection of ideas for teatime treats:

SAVOURY

Dainty sandwiches, cut into small triangles without crusts. You can make any fillings you like, but some popular choices are cucumber, egg or poached salmon.

SWEET

Fresh scones and a selection of delicious mini cakes, such as fruitcake, macaroons, carrot cake, brownies and banana bread muffins.

Cream and jam for the scones – ideally served in separate little pots, one of each for every guest, if possible.

CROCKERY

An assortment of chintzy teapots, china teacups (with saucers), milk jug, sugar bowl and plates. A layered cake stand will make for a lovely presentation.

TEA

Stock up on English breakfast tea, Earl Grey, peppermint, chamomile, jasmine and any other varieties that take your fancy. Pink champagne is an optional extra.

LEMON, GINGER AND HONEY TEA

This is the perfect pick-me-up when you are feeling a bit run down.
Lemon and ginger boost your immune system and help you fight off colds,
while the honey soothes and comforts.

SERVES 1

2-cm piece of root ginger, sliced or grated
250 ml freshly boiled water
juice of 1 lemon
1 tablespoon honey

Place the ginger in a teapot, pour
in the freshly boiled water and leave
the ginger to steep for 5 minutes.

Place the lemon juice and honey
in a mug, then strain the ginger tea
into the mug, stirring to dissolve
the honey.

SPICED CHAI TEA

Originally from India, chai tea has become a favourite in cafés around the world. Spice blends vary but almost always include ginger and cardamom, both of which add a lovely warmth.

SERVES 4

2.5-cm piece of root ginger, roughly chopped
1 cinnamon stick, broken into short pieces
¾ teaspoon fennel seeds
3 cloves
6 cardamom pods
4 English breakfast teabags
125 ml milk
honey or sugar, to taste

Bring 1 litre of water to the boil in a small saucepan. Add the ginger and the spices, and simmer for 10 minutes. Add the teabags to the saucepan and simmer for another 4 minutes.

Warm the milk in a separate saucepan and pour it into the tea. Heat the mixture for 2 minutes more and strain into four teacups. Add honey or sugar to taste.

ICED GREEN TEA

SERVES 4

Small handful fresh mint
3 teaspoons of green tea leaves
2 tablespoons runny honey

Finely chop the mint. Steep all the ingredients in 900 ml of boiling water for 5 minutes, strain the tea leaves and chill before serving.

PEPPERMINT TEA

Both caffeine- and calorie-free, peppermint tea is known to aid digestion, which makes it particularly soothing to drink after a meal. You can make yourself a cup simply using leaves grown in your own garden.

SERVES 1

1 heaped teaspoon dried mint leaves or
  2 sprigs of fresh mint
250 ml freshly boiled water
honey or sugar, to taste

Place the mint in a teapot, pour in the freshly boiled water and leave the mint to steep for 5 to 10 minutes.

Pour the tea through a strainer into a mug and add honey or sugar to taste.

Treat yourself and others to a leisurely homemade brunch with these lovely ideas. Includes quirky takes on classic recipes to impress family and friends. Serve with strongly brewed coffee or a large pot of English breakfast tea. Delicious, quick and healthy recipes are also included if you want something a bit special during the week or lighter options for brunch.

Breakfast Blast

Good Morning Juice

Mojito Fruit Salad

Honey Banana Smoothie

Papaya and Yogurt Smoothie

Strawberry Milkshake

French Toast

Fruity Teabread

Crunchy Pear and
Cinnamon Muffins

Cherry Almond Granola

Raisin and Cinnamon Rolls

Almond Porridge with Compote

Strawberry and Peach Compote

Perfect Pancakes

Chestnut Pancakes
with Pomegranate

LUSCIOUS
BRUNCH

BREAKFAST BLAST

Enjoy this fast, but, substantial breakfast in a glass when time is short in the morning. The kale in this recipe gives you a great boost of fibre, folate and vitamins A, C and K.

SERVES 1
250 ml apple juice
100 g kale
100 g raspberries or blueberries
50 g rolled oats
½ banana, peeled
2 medjool dates

Place all the ingredients in a blender and blitz well. For more liquid, use cold water to dilute. Leave for 5 minutes to macerate before serving.

GOOD MORNING JUICE

SERVES 1
½ grapefruit, peeled
1 lemon, peeled
2 celery sticks
½ cucumber, peeled
3 red radishes
1 red apple, quartered
2.5-cm piece of root ginger, peeled

Juice the grapefruit, lemon, celery and cucumber. Add the radishes to the juicer – if the radish leaves are still fresh and green they can go in there, too. Add the apple and root ginger to the juicer. Mix all the juices together, then pour into a glass to serve.

MOJITO FRUIT SALAD

Mojito does not have to be a drink or even contain alcohol. This salad packs its own pick-me-up punch. The mint and limes in this salad bring a delicious freshness to your morning.

SERVES 4

100 g watermelon, rind removed
2 ripe mangoes, peeled and pitted
100 g pineapple, rind removed
grated zest and juice of 3 limes
bunch of mint

Slice the watermelon, mangoes and pineapple into equal sizes, taking care to keep the juice. Add the zest and juice of the limes. Arrange the fruit on a plate, pour over the juice and decorate with mint.

HONEY BANANA SMOOTHIE

SERVES 4

1 ripe banana
350 ml milk or non-dairy alternative
1 to 2 tablespoons honey or maple syrup
¼ teaspoon ground nutmeg
3 ice cubes

Place all the ingredients in a blender and blend until smooth. Serve immediately as a satisfying breakfast.

Alternatively, omit the ice cubes and add a little more milk to the blended mixture. Transfer to a saucepan, warm gently and serve in heatproof glasses topped with a sprinkle of freshly ground nutmeg.

PAPAYA AND YOGURT SMOOTHIE

SERVES 1

15 g walnuts, coarsely ground
2 tablespoons linseeds, coarsely ground
200 g yogurt
30 ml linseed oil
1 teaspoon agave syrup
lemon or orange juice
100 g papaya, peeled and diced

Place the ground walnuts and linseeds in a glass bowl with the yogurt, linseed oil and agave syrup. Stir and season with a squeeze of lemon or orange juice. Lay the diced papaya on top.

STRAWBERRY MILKSHAKE FRENCH TOAST

SERVES 3

250 ml strawberry milk

3 eggs

1 teaspoon vanilla extract

60 g butter, plus extra for frying

20 strawberries

6 slices of day-old brioche bread

60 g caster sugar

Mix the strawberry milk, eggs and vanilla extract together in a large dish. Melt the butter and whisk it into the mixture.

Slice some of the strawberries. Cut a pocket in each piece of bread and insert some strawberry slices. Dip the bread into the milkshake and leave for a minute so that the bread soaks it up, then flip over and repeat on the other side.

Heat a frying pan and add some butter. Place a slice of the soaked bread into the pan and fry on each side for 3 minutes until cooked and nicely browned.

Chop the remaining strawberries and add to a saucepan with the sugar and 1 tablespoon of water. Boil over a low heat for about 10 minutes until you get a thick syrup. Press the syrup through a sieve, then pour it over the French toast and enjoy.

FRUITY TEABREAD

Teabreads are traditional English cakes made with mixed dried fruit soaked overnight in black tea. Dense and moist, they are best baked in loaf tins and served sliced and buttered.

SERVES 8

225 g mixed dried fruit
225 ml freshly made black tea
butter, for greasing
225 g self-raising flour
115 g brown sugar
1 egg, beaten
2 tablespoons orange marmalade

Place the dried fruit in a large bowl, pour the black tea over the top and leave overnight to soak.

Preheat the oven to 180°C. Grease a 700-g loaf tin and base-line with baking paper.

Sift the flour into a large bowl and stir in the sugar. Add the beaten egg to the dry ingredients along with the marmalade, the soaked fruit and any remaining soaking liquid. Mix thoroughly.

Spoon the teabread mixture into the prepared loaf tin, smooth the top and bake for 1 hour until a skewer inserted into the cake comes out clean.

Leave to cool in the tin for 10 minutes before turning out onto a wire rack. Peel off the baking paper and leave to cool completely before slicing.

CRUNCHY PEAR AND CINNAMON MUFFINS

These quick and simple muffins are a delightful combination of warming spice and sweet pears, and make a delicious mid-morning snack. Apples are a good substitute if you do not have pears to hand. Pecans and walnuts are recommended in this recipe but almonds and/or hazelnuts can also be used.

MAKES 12

60 ml vegetable oil, plus extra
 for greasing
200 g plain flour
2 teaspoons baking powder
150 g soft brown sugar
½ teaspoon salt
3 teaspoons ground cinnamon
1 egg, beaten
60 ml milk
2 pears, peeled and chopped
1 tablespoon pecans or walnuts, chopped
2 tablespoons demerara sugar

Preheat the oven to 200°C. Grease a 12-hole muffin tin or line with paper cases.

Sift the flour and baking powder together into a large mixing bowl and stir in the brown sugar, salt and two teaspoons of the cinnamon.

Combine the beaten egg with the oil and milk. Pour into the flour and mix until just combined. Fold in the chopped pears. Spoon the batter into the prepared muffin tin. Mix the chopped nuts into the demerara sugar and the remaining cinnamon, and sprinkle over the muffins.

Bake for 20 minutes, or until well risen and cooked through.

CHERRY ALMOND GRANOLA

SERVES 4

300 g rolled oats
2 tablespoons pumpkin seeds
2 tablespoons sunflower seeds
2 tablespoons sesame seeds
200 g flaked almonds
1 teaspoon almond essence
125 ml maple syrup
2 tablespoons rapeseed oil
100 g dried cherries

Preheat the oven to 150°C. Line a baking sheet with baking paper.

Mix all the ingredients together, except for the dried cherries. Spread the mixture over the prepared baking sheet and bake for 15 minutes.

Stir up the mixture, adding in the dried cherries, and return to the oven for up to 15 minutes more, until golden. Tip onto a cold baking sheet to cool – the granola will crisp up more. Store in an airtight container for up to one month.

RAISIN AND CINNAMON ROLLS

Indulge in this delicious treat as a morning snack or as part of a high tea in the afternoon. If you are short of time the uncooked rolls can be left covered in the refrigerator overnight and baked the next day.

MAKES 16

450 g strong white flour, plus extra
*   for dusting*
1 tablespoon ground cinnamon
1½ teaspoons fast-action dried yeast
50 g caster sugar
½ teaspoon salt
180 ml warm milk
2 large eggs
90 g unsalted butter, melted
150 g raisins
1 tablespoon each of granulated sugar and
*   boiling water, to glaze*

Sift the flour and cinnamon into a large bowl. Add the yeast, caster sugar and salt.

Whisk together the milk, eggs and butter, pour over the flour and mix to a soft dough. Knead until silky and elastic. Form the dough into a ball, cover and leave to rise for about 1½ hours until doubled in volume.

On a lightly floured board, pat the dough into a 30 x 20 cm rectangle. Sprinkle with the raisins then, starting from one long edge, roll the dough into a log. Cut into 16 slices and place the pinwheels of dough on greased and floured baking sheets, spacing them well apart. Cover with a tea towel and leave to rise again. Meanwhile, preheat the oven to 200°C.

Bake the rolls for 25 minutes. Transfer to a rack and glaze the tops with granulated sugar dissolved in hot water while the rolls are still hot.

ALMOND PORRIDGE WITH COMPOTE

A big bowl of home-made porridge is the perfect way to warm up on a cold winter's day. The chia seeds and quinoa make this a light version that can be enjoyed all year round.

SERVES 1
40 g almonds
1 tablespoon hempseeds
1 tablespoon flaxseeds
40 g quinoa
40 g oats
1 tablespoon chia seeds
berries and coconut flakes, to serve

Blend the almonds, hempseeds and flaxseeds with 100 ml of cold water. Transfer to a small saucepan with the quinoa, oats and chia seeds. Heat gently, stirring, to make a porridge-like mix, adding a little more water if needed.

Serve with fresh berries and dried coconut flakes.

STRAWBERRY AND PEACH COMPOTE

SERVES 1
1 ripe peach, halved and diced
6 strawberries, quartered

Mix the peach with the strawberries, adding any juices you have caught. Leave to infuse for 5 minutes before serving.

PERFECT PANCAKES

Pancakes are a special breakfast or brunch treat that are simple and fun to make. Popular toppings include sugar and lemon, strawberry jam, banana slices and chocolate spread.

MAKES 8
1 egg
280 ml milk
110 g plain flour
pinch of salt
1 tablespoon vegetable or sunflower oil
toppings of your choice

In a large bowl, whisk the egg into the milk.

Sift the flour and salt into a second large bowl, and gradually add the egg and milk mixture, stirring vigorously to avoid lumps forming. The batter should be runny and creamy. Add a drop of oil to a heavy-based frying pan and place on the stove over a high heat. Add two large spoonfuls of batter and tilt the pan until it is thinly, but evenly, coated.

The first side only takes about 1 minute to cook. When it's done, flip the pancake and cook the other side.

Slide the pancake onto a plate and add a topping of your choice.

CHESTNUT PANCAKES WITH POMEGRANATE

MAKES 8

50 g chestnut flour
50 g spelt flour
2 large eggs
pinch of sea salt flakes
240 ml milk
60 ml water
1 tablespoon melted butter
1 tablespoon vegetable or sunflower oil

for the filling

250 g ricotta cheese
1 teaspoon agave syrup
125 g pomegranate seeds
berries, to decorate

Place the pancake ingredients in a blender and blend until smooth. Pour into a bowl, cover and rest for 1 hour at room temperature.

Add a drop of oil to a warm nonstick frying pan and cook the pancakes in batches for 1 minute each side.

For the filling, mash the ricotta with the agave syrup and mix in the pomegranate seeds. Spread onto the pancakes and stack or fold into squares. Decorate with berries.

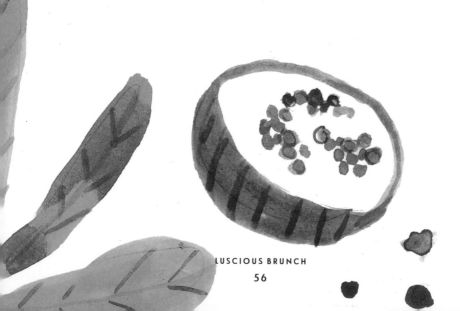

Pottering around in the kitchen is a delightful pastime all year round, but during the holidays or on special occasions it can sometimes be a little stressful. Ordered by season these simple and traditional recipes take the fuss out of the festivities and provide you with the perfect ideas for all occasions.

FESTIVE
TREATS

HOT CROSS BUN CUPCAKES

MAKES 12

3 large eggs, beaten
90 ml buttermilk
185 g unsalted butter, melted
grated zest of 1 orange
185 g self-raising flour
½ teaspoon baking powder
70 g almond meal
185 g light brown sugar
2 teaspoons mixed spice
120 g sultanas
1 tablespoon apricot jam

for the icing

60 g cream cheese
40 g unsalted butter
60 g icing sugar
grated zest of ½ orange

Preheat the oven to 180°C. Grease a 12-hole cupcake tin or line with paper cases.

Beat the eggs in a bowl and then add the buttermilk. Melt the butter, add it to the bowl and mix well. Stir in the orange zest.

In a separate bowl, sift together the flour, baking powder, almond meal, sugar and mixed spice. Fold these into the wet mixture, then stir in the sultanas.

Spoon the cake batter into the cupcake tin, about three-quarters full, and bake for 18 to 20 minutes until a skewer comes out clean.

Heat the apricot jam in a small saucepan with a dash of cold water. Using a pastry brush, glaze the cakes while they are still warm and then allow to cool.

To make the icing, mix all the ingredients together. Spoon the mixture into a piping bag with a small plain nozzle and pipe a cross onto the top of each cake.

ICED EASTER BISCUITS

Get creative when decorating these festive treats, using different colours, patterns and shapes. These biscuits are lovely at any time of the year, just use different cutter shapes and colours and voila, you have Christmas or Halloween biscuits.

MAKES 30

425 g plain flour, plus extra for dusting
½ teaspoon salt
200 g caster sugar
225 g unsalted butter
2 eggs
½ teaspoon almond or vanilla essence

for the icing

170 g icing sugar
juice of 2 lemons
food colouring (optional)

Preheat the oven to 180°C. Line two baking sheets with baking paper.

Combine the flour, salt and caster sugar in a large bowl. Rub in the butter until the mixture resembles fine breadcrumbs. Add the yolks of the two eggs and just one white, along with the flavouring. Bring everything together to form a soft dough. Chill for 1 hour.

On a lightly floured board, roll out the dough to a thickness of about 5 mm. Use Easter cutters in egg, bunny and chick shapes to stamp out biscuits. Lay them, well spaced, on the prepared baking sheets and bake for 10 minutes, or until lightly coloured. Cool for 5 minutes before transferring them to a wire rack.

To make the icing, mix the icing sugar with enough lemon juice and colouring to make a smooth paste. Using a piping bag and small nozzle, decorate the biscuits with patterns of zigzags, scallops, spots and dots. Allow the icing to dry before storing the biscuits in an airtight container.

CREAMY VANILLA ICE CREAM

Ice cream is an essential part of summer and making your own at home is an absolute delight. Add chocolate pieces, nuts, sweets or fresh berries for extra indulgence.

SERVES 4

4 eggs, separated
110 g caster sugar
300 ml whipping cream
vanilla essence

Whisk the egg yolks in a bowl until they are blended. Whisk the egg whites in a separate, larger bowl, either by hand or using an electric mixer, until they form soft peaks. Whisk the sugar in with the egg whites, one teaspoon at a time. The whites will get stiffer as the sugar is added. Blend in the egg yolks until no streaks of colour remain. Whisk the cream until it forms soft peaks and then fold into the egg mixture, adding a few drops of vanilla essence.

Pour the mixture into a large plastic container, cover and freeze. Stir the mixture every so often to break up the ice crystals.

SUMMER FRUIT TART

Is there a more luscious way to utilize an abundance of summer fruit?

SERVES 6

100 g apricot jam
1 sweet pastry case (see p. 24)

for the filling

1 large egg, plus 1 egg yolk
55 g caster sugar
25 g plain flour
300 ml milk
few drops of vanilla essence
600 g mixed summer fruits: strawberries, raspberries, blueberries, kiwifruit, mandarin or orange segments

Spoon the jam into a small saucepan with 1 tablespoon of cold water and heat gently, stirring, to make a syrup. Use a pastry brush to coat the base of the pastry case with the syrup and leave to cool. This will help to keep the base of the tart crisp.

To make the filling, beat the egg and egg yolk with the sugar, then gradually beat in the flour and milk. Transfer the mixture to a small saucepan and bring to the boil, whisking continuously. Simmer for about 3 minutes, then remove from the heat and stir in the vanilla essence. Pour the mixture into a shallow dish to cool, and stir occasionally to prevent a skin from forming.

Pour the filling into the pastry case and cover with a decorative arrangement of your chosen fruit.

Brush the fruit with the remaining syrup and serve at room temperature.

TANGY LEMONADE

Homemade lemonade is far superior to the commercial variety and is super simple to make. Whip up this refreshing beverage on a hot summer's day.

SERVES 6

240 g caster sugar (according to taste)
250 ml hot water
250 ml lemon juice
ice cubes
lemon slices

Dissolve the sugar in the hot water by heating it in a small saucepan over a low heat. The resulting mixture is known as sugar syrup. Pour the sugar syrup into a jug and add the lemon juice. Add about 1 litre of cold water until the mixture reaches the desired strength.

Chill the lemonade in the refrigerator for 30 to 40 minutes.

Serve with ice and a slice of lemon.

REFRESHING CRANBERRY JUICE

SERVES 8

450 g cranberries
pinch of salt
3 orange slices (optional)
100 g caster sugar

Wash the cranberries and place them in a saucepan with 1.2 litres of cold water, the salt and orange slices, if using.

Cook over a medium heat until all the berries burst. This should take about 10 minutes.

Pour the fruit and liquid into a cheesecloth-lined sieve and strain the juice back into the saucepan. Add the sugar and boil for 2 to 3 minutes. Taste and add more sugar if needed.

Leave to cool and then chill the juice before serving.

TOFFEE APPLES

MAKES 8

8 granny smith apples, stalks removed
500 g golden caster sugar
2 teaspoons malt vinegar
80 g golden syrup
8 wooden skewers or lollypop sticks

Place the apples in a large bowl and cover with boiling water. This is to remove any waxy coating and help the caramel stick. Dry thoroughly and push a skewer or stick into the stalk end of each apple.

Place the apples on a sheet of baking paper. Tip the sugar into a pan along with 100 ml cold water and set over a medium heat. Cook for 5 minutes until the sugar is dissolved, then stir in the vinegar and golden syrup. Boil until it reaches 'hard crack' stage (150°C on a sugar thermometer). Test by pouring a little into a bowl of cold water. It should harden instantly into brittle threads that are easy to break. Continue to boil if the toffee is still malleable.

Working quickly and carefully, dip and twist each apple in the hot toffee until covered, letting any excess drip away and place on the baking paper to harden. (You may have to heat the toffee a little if the temperature drops and it starts to feel thick and sticky.) Leave to cool completely.

The toffee apples should last for two days when stored in a cool dry place.

PUMPKIN PIE

This is a classic North American recipe that is traditionally served at Thanksgiving and Christmas. The spices complement the pumpkin beautifully.

SERVES 6

750 g pumpkin or butternut squash,
*   peeled and cubed*
300 g fresh or frozen sweet
*   shortcrust pastry*
2 large eggs
170 g soft brown sugar
1 teaspoon ground cinnamon
½ teaspoon each ground ginger and nutmeg
½ teaspoon salt
120 ml double cream or evaporated milk,
*   plus extra cream to serve*

Preheat the oven to 180°C. Place the pumpkin or squash in a large saucepan, cover with cold water and bring to the boil. Simmer for 10 minutes, or until tender. Drain and return to the saucepan. Dry over a low heat before sieving the flesh into a bowl. Leave to cool.

Line a 23-cm pie dish or tart tin with the pastry. Line the pastry with a piece of crumpled nonstick baking paper weighted with rice or baking beans. Bake the shell for 15 minutes, then remove the paper and weights.

While the pastry is baking, combine the pumpkin purée with the eggs, sugar, spices, salt and cream or evaporated milk, and mix well. Taste and add more spice if needed. Carefully pour the mixture into the par-cooked pastry shell and bake for 45 to 50 minutes, or until just set. Serve hot or warm with cream.

SCANDINAVIAN MULLED WINE

This Scandinavian-style mulled wine, known as glögg *definitely packs a punch! Traditionally, it is served with raisins, which are put into the bottom of the glasses before filling up. Leave teaspoons next to the punchbowl so guests can spoon the fruit out and eat it once they've finished drinking.*

SERVES 6
60 ml vodka
1 cinnamon stick
5 cloves
750 ml fruity red wine
1 teaspoon ground cinnamon
½ teaspoon ground ginger
115 g brown sugar

Pour the vodka into a large saucepan and add the cinnamon stick and cloves. Bring to simmering point and then set aside for at least 1 hour.

When your guests arrive, pour in the wine and add the ground cinnamon, ginger and sugar. Serve warm.

ALCOHOL-FREE BLUEBERRY AND GINGER CUP

SERVES 3
2 handfuls of blueberries
30 ml fresh lemon juice
45 ml vanilla extract
30 ml sugar syrup
30 ml fresh ginger juice
ice, cubed and crushed
250 ml cranberry juice
extra blueberries and lemon slices,
  to decorate

Put the blueberries and the lemon juice in a cocktail shaker and muddle. Followed by the vanilla, sugar and ginger. Add ice cubes and shake well. Half fill glasses with crushed ice and strain the shaken mixture into the glass. Pour the cranberry juice into the glasses, stir well, top with more crushed ice and blueberries and a lemon slice.

TRADITIONAL HOT TODDY

Chase away a sore throat and warm your soul on a cold winter's evening. Any whisky can be used but there's no point breaking out your best single malt for this winter warmer, as the subtle flavours would be wasted.

SERVES 1
1 to 2 tablespoons honey
1 lemon slice
a few cloves (optional)
allspice or cinnamon stick (optional)
a strong spirit, such as whisky

Half-fill a glass with just-boiled water. Placing a spoon in the glass and pouring the water over that will help to prevent the glass cracking from the heat; otherwise heat the glass slightly before adding the water. Stir in a spoonful or two of honey. Add half a lemon slice studded with two to four cloves. If you want a strong citrus flavour, squeeze in the juice of the other half of the lemon slice.

If desired, add a pinch of allspice or a cinnamon stick for extra kick.

Finally, add a good glug of whisky to taste.

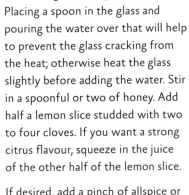

SPICED CIDER

This is the perfect drink for celebrating Halloween or Christmas. You can keep the saucepan warm for quite a few hours at a low heat. Then people can refill their glasses throughout the evening.

SERVES 8
1 litre cider
3 tablespoons brown sugar
rind of 1 orange
1 apple, thinly sliced
2 to 3 cinnamon sticks
handful of cloves
2 teaspoons ground allspice
80 ml brandy
extra cinnamon sticks and orange slices,
 for decoration

Place all the ingredients in a saucepan.

Heat gently for approximately 20 minutes, stirring occasionally and ensuring that all the sugar has dissolved. Do not boil, as this would burn off the alcohol and may turn the spices slightly bitter.

When ready, strain into glasses or cups, garnish with extra cinnamon sticks or orange slices, and enjoy.

LEBKUCHEN

This traditional German Christmas treat is similar to gingerbread and often used to decorate stalls at German-style Christmas markets.

MAKES 24

180 ml runny honey
225 g light muscovado sugar
60 g unsalted butter
450 g plain flour
½ teaspoon bicarbonate of soda
1½ teaspoons each of ground ginger and cinnamon
½ teaspoon each of ground nutmeg and cardamom
2 large eggs, beaten
150 g currants
120 g chopped candied peel
100 g chopped almonds
zest of 1 lemon, finely grated

for the icing

55 g icing sugar
1 tablespoon boiling water
few drops of lemon juice

Line a shallow 30 x 20 cm baking tin with baking paper.

Gently heat, without boiling, the honey, sugar and butter, stirring until the sugar has dissolved. Sift together the flour, bicarbonate of soda and spices. Combine the flour and honey mixture with the eggs, dried fruit, nuts and lemon zest.

Press the dough evenly into the tin, cover and chill – ideally for 48 hours – before baking.

Preheat the oven to 180°C. Uncover the dough and bake for 35 minutes, or until golden brown and firm.

Mix the icing ingredients together and brush over the warm cake. Cool the cake in its tin before turning out. Peel off the baking paper and cut the cake into 5-cm squares.

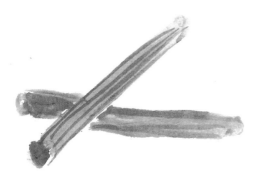

TRADITIONAL GERMAN STOLLEN

*Buttery, filled with fruit and finished with a dusting of sugar, stollen is
a cake-like bread and a traditional part of a German Christmas. A range of
dried fruit can be used but it always includes currants, raisins and candied
citrus peel. Serve with mulled wine for added festive cheer.*

MAKES 2 LOAVES

150 g raisins
200 g mixed candied peel
200 g glacé cherries
100 ml rum
1 kg strong white flour
1 tablespoon fast-action dried yeast
225 g caster sugar
½ teaspoon salt
300 ml warm milk
2 large eggs
1 teaspoon almond essence
*280 g unsalted butter, softened, plus extra
 for greasing*
100 g chopped almonds
50 g icing sugar

Soak the raisins, mixed peel and cherries in the rum overnight. Drain, reserving the rum.

In a large bowl, combine the flour, yeast, caster sugar and salt. Whisk the reserved rum with the milk, eggs and almond essence. Pour this liquid into the flour mixture and work in two-thirds of the butter to make a soft dough. Knead until smooth and elastic before incorporating the fruit and nuts. Cover and leave to rise until doubled in volume.

Divide the dough in two, and roll each half into a rectangle measuring approximately 30 x 20 cm. Melt the remaining butter and brush on both strips of dough. To shape the loaves, fold one long edge to the centre. Fold the opposite edge to overlap the centre by 2.5 cm. Set the loaves well apart on a buttered baking sheet, brush the tops with butter and leave to rise until doubled in volume again.

Preheat the oven to 190°C and bake the loaves for about 45 minutes. Transfer them to a wire rack and, while they are still warm, brush with the remaining melted butter and dredge with the icing sugar. Stollen should mature for at least three days in an airtight container before eating.

FESTIVE EGGNOG

*A spicy, creamy, boozy Christmas treat that can also be made with rum
or bourbon. Add a splash of Madeira wine for a spicy, festive and slightly
currant warmth.*

SERVES 8
4 egg yolks
100 g caster sugar
475 ml whole milk
pinch of ground cinnamon
1 vanilla bean
240 ml double cream
200 ml brandy
1 teaspoon freshly grated nutmeg

In a large bowl, whisk the egg yolks until they become pale in colour, and then add the sugar in four parts, beating in between, so the mixture becomes light and fluffy.

Pour the milk into a saucepan and add the cinnamon and vanilla bean. Warm over a medium heat until the milk goes frothy and is just about to boil. Remove the milk from the heat and pour a splash of it into the egg mixture, then stir. Add a little more, then stir again, and finally, pour it all in. Adding the milk to the eggs, and not vice versa, means you won't get scrambled eggs!

Pour everything back into the saucepan and return to the heat. Stir constantly until the mixture thickens and coats the back of a wooden spoon (about 10 minutes). Make sure it doesn't boil.

Remove from the heat and discard the vanilla bean. Stir in the double cream, let your mixture cool for an hour, then pour in the brandy and chill.

Sprinkle with freshly grated nutmeg before serving.

HOT CHOCOLATE

A delicious treat for chocolate lovers, this recipe works perfectly with dark or milk chocolate, or a mix of both, depending on how chocolatey you like it. A pinch of cinnamon can also be added for a warming spice kick.

SERVES 2

170 g chocolate, chopped

500 ml milk

Boil a little water in a saucepan, then turn the heat down to a simmer. Place the chocolate in a heat-resistant bowl and place the bowl over the saucepan, making sure it does not touch the bottom. Stir the chocolate occasionally until it has melted into a smooth consistency.

Put the melted chocolate to one side while you heat the milk in a saucepan over a low flame. Keep an eye on the chocolate to make sure it doesn't harden.

Add the chocolate to the milk, mixing well.

Giving thoughtful gifts that you have made yourself is a wonderful way to make the lucky recipient feel extra special and pampered. These treats are suitable for all occasions and will satisfy the sweet tooth in everyone — but it is also perfectly acceptable to keep these delicious sweets all to yourself!

SWEET
GIFTS

PERFECT FUDGE

This melt-in-the-mouth fudge makes a lovely gift for any occasion. Once you have mastered this basic recipe get creative with different flavours and colours. The flavour combinations for fudge are virtually endless making this a lovely gift, which can be tailored specifically for individual recipients.

MAKES 1.2 KG

100 g unsalted butter, plus extra
 for greasing
680 g granulated sugar
400 g sweetened condensed milk
¼ teaspoon salt
1 teaspoon vanilla bean paste

Grease a 20-cm square tin.

Put the butter, sugar, 180 ml of cold water, condensed milk and salt in a heavy-based saucepan and heat gently until the sugar dissolves. Use a pastry brush dipped in water to wash down any sugar crystals from the sides of the saucepan. Raise the heat and boil the syrup to the soft-ball stage (116°C on a sugar thermometer).

Take the saucepan off the heat and dip the base in cold water. Rest for 2 minutes before adding the vanilla and beating the syrup with a wooden spoon until it starts to stiffen. Immediately pour it into the prepared tin and mark it into squares. When cold, cut the fudge into pieces. Store in an airtight container.

PISTACHIO AND CARDAMOM FUDGE

Replace the vanilla with ½ teaspoon of freshly ground cardamom seeds and 100 g of chopped pistachios, added to the syrup before beating it.

RAISIN AND PECAN FUDGE

Add 75 g of raisins and 100 g of chopped pecans to the syrup before beating it.

EASY VEGAN FUDGE

MAKES 50

700 g caster sugar
600 ml soya milk
115 g vegan margarine
2 teaspoons vanilla essence

Line an 18-cm square tin with baking paper. Half-fill the kitchen sink with cold water.

Place the sugar, soya milk and margarine in a large saucepan, and heat gently to melt the margarine and dissolve the sugar. Bring to the boil and simmer until the temperature reaches 120°C on a sugar thermometer.

If you don't have a sugar thermometer, prepare a small bowl of cold water. When the mixture is ready, a little of it dropped into the water will form a soft ball. Quickly stir in the vanilla essence, then carefully take the saucepan off the heat and put it into the cold water in the kitchen sink to cool the mixture down quickly. Beat the mixture with a wooden spoon until it becomes very thick, then pour it into the prepared tin, smooth the top and leave at room temperature to set.

When the fudge is firm, remove it from the tin and cut it into small pieces using a sharp knife.

ORANGE BLOSSOM MARSHMALLOWS

MAKES 80

450 g granulated sugar
1 tablespoon liquid glucose
8 gelatine leaves
2 large egg whites
2 teaspoons orange flower water, to taste
a few drops of orange food colouring,
  to taste
icing sugar and cornflour, to dust

Base-line a shallow 30 x 20 cm cake tin with baking paper and dust with cornflour.

Place the sugar in a large saucepan with the glucose and 240 ml of cold water. Heat gently until the sugar dissolves. Wash down any sugar crystals from the sides of the saucepan using a pastry brush dipped in water. Raise the heat and boil the syrup to the hard-ball stage (121°C on a sugar thermometer). While the syrup is cooking, soak the gelatine in cold water for 5 minutes and whisk the egg whites to stiff peaks.

Take the syrup off the heat. Squeeze the excess water out of the softened gelatine and stir it into the syrup. Whisking continuously, pour the syrup into the meringue in a thin, steady stream until the mixture forms a dense cloud of marshmallow. Whisk in a little orange flower water and colouring to taste.

Pour the marshmallow into the prepared tin. When set, cut into cubes, discs or hearts, and dust lightly on all sides with a 50–50 mixture of cornflour and icing sugar.

Offcuts can be used up in Rocky Road Bites (p. 91).

PINK ROSE MARSHMALLOWS

Add rosewater and red food colouring.

COFFEE MARSHMALLOWS

Add coffee essence or very strong espresso to the mixture.

TOFFEE NUT POPCORN

MAKES 250 G

75 g shelled and skinned hazelnuts
1 tablespoon vegetable oil, plus extra
 for greasing
65 g popping corn
60 g butter
½ teaspoon salt
60 ml golden syrup

Preheat the oven to 180°C. Spread the nuts on a baking sheet and toast them for about 10 minutes, until lightly browned. Cool before chopping coarsely. Set aside.

Pour the oil into a large saucepan with a tight-fitting lid. Heat until the oil shimmers, add the corn and cover with a lid. Holding the lid on and shaking the saucepan cook the corn over a high heat until all popping sounds stop. Transfer the popped corn into a large bowl and add the reserved nuts.

In the hot saucepan, heat the butter, salt and syrup, stirring until they are combined. Bubble the mixture briskly for 5 minutes before adding the popcorn and nuts. Stir quickly to coat the popcorn evenly.

Turn out on to a lightly greased baking sheet to cool and crisp up. Store in an airtight container if you can resist eating it all at once.

BUTTERED SALTED POPCORN

Replace the nuts and golden syrup with an extra ½ teaspoon of salt.

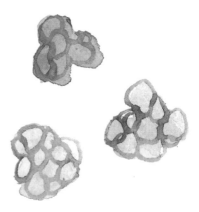

ENGLISH MADELEINES

These adorable cakes are similar to the Australian lamington but are brushed with jam not chocolate. Dariole moulds are suggested but silicone cake moulds or even a humble muffin tin can be used instead.

MAKES 6

90 g butter
110 g caster sugar
2 eggs
1 teaspoon vanilla extract
100 g self-raising flour
1 teaspoon baking powder
60 g raspberry jam
90 g desiccated coconut

Preheat the oven to 180°C. Grease each dariole mould and line the bottom with baking paper.

Cream the butter and sugar until pale and creamy. Beat in the eggs one at a time, then stir in the vanilla extract. Sift in the flour and baking powder and fold into the mixture.

Fill each mould a little over half full with the cake mixture. Bake for 20–25 minutes until firm and golden, then remove from the moulds and allow to cool.

Slice the risen tops off the cakes to give a flat surface and turn upside down.

Press the jam through a sieve into a saucepan. Warm the jam and brush some onto each cake. Roll the cakes in coconut, using a fork to hold them.

COCONUT ICE SQUARES

MAKES 50
oil, for greasing
450 g granulated sugar
180 ml half-fat tinned coconut milk
180 g desiccated coconut

Grease a shallow, 20-cm square
cake tin.

Place the sugar in a heavy-based
saucepan with the coconut milk
and heat slowly until the sugar has
dissolved completely. Wash down any
sugar crystals from the sides of the
saucepan with a pastry brush dipped
in cold water. Raise the heat and
boil the syrup to the soft-ball stage
(116°C on a sugar thermometer).

Stir in the desiccated coconut and
immediately pour the mixture into
the prepared tin. When it starts to
stiffen, mark it into squares.

When completely cold, turn
the slab out and cut it into the
marked squares.

TRADITIONAL PINK AND WHITE COCONUT ICE

Pour half the white coconut ice into
the tin. Add a few drops of red food
colouring to the remainder and pour
this mix over the white layer.

CARDAMOM COCONUT ICE

Add 2 teaspoons of freshly ground
cardamom seeds to the dessicated
coconut before mixing it with the
syrup. Dust each square in more
desiccated coconut to finish.

DECADENT CHOCOLATE TRUFFLES

Impress friends and family with these wicked chocolate treats. Ideally, you should use chocolate with a 70 per cent cocoa content. The truffles will keep in an airtight container for three days, or freeze for a month.

MAKES 50
280 g dark chocolate, chopped small
284 ml double cream
50 g unsalted butter
pinch of sea salt flakes

Place the chocolate pieces in a large bowl.

Place the cream and butter in a saucepan and heat gently, so that the butter melts and the cream simmers. Remove the saucepan from the heat and pour the mixture over the chocolate pieces. Stir, so that the chocolate melts and you get a glossy smooth mixture. Add the salt.

If you want to flavour the truffles, add your preferred flavouring now: try 2 tablespoons of brandy, Grand Marnier or coconut rum; the zest and juice of an orange; a tablespoon of chopped crystallized ginger; or a teaspoon of chilli.

Leave the mixture to cool, then chill in the refrigerator for at least 2 hours.

To shape the truffles into balls, dip a dessertspoon or melon baller into a cup of boiling water and it will easily glide through the chocolate mixture.

To decorate the truffles, roll them in toasted dried coconut or flaked almonds, or sprinkle with cocoa powder or crystallized ginger. To coat them in chocolate, melt pieces of chocolate in a bowl over a saucepan of boiling water. Allow to cool slightly, then spoon over the truffles until well coated. Leave to cool and harden.

PEANUT BUTTER TRUFFLES

MAKES 18 TO 20

115 g dates, finely chopped
115 g walnuts, finely chopped
115 g icing sugar
225 g vegan peanut butter
  (smooth or crunchy)
115 g vegan plain chocolate,
  roughly chopped
grated chocolate, to decorate

Mix the dates and walnuts with the icing sugar and peanut butter. Roll into truffle-sized balls and place on a baking sheet lined with baking paper.

Chill for up to 20 minutes.

Melt the chocolate in a small heatproof bowl over a saucepan of hot water.

Using a toothpick, dip the truffles into the melted chocolate, carefully returning them to the baking paper. Sprinkle the truffles with a little grated chocolate. Return to the refrigerator until the chocolate has set firmly.

SALTED BUTTER CARAMELS

These vintage sweets should be soft, chewy and melt-in-your-mouth. For an added touch, wrap them in cellophane and present to family and friends in cute decorated boxes.

MAKES 64

45 g butter, plus extra for greasing
225 g soft brown sugar
250 ml double cream
60 ml runny honey
1½ teaspoons salt
1 teaspoon vanilla essence

Grease a shallow, 20-cm square cake tin and base-line it with baking paper.

Place the butter, sugar, cream, honey and salt into a heavy-based saucepan and heat gently, stirring until the sugar dissolves completely.

Wash down any sugar crystals from the sides of the saucepan with a pastry brush dipped in cold water. Raise the heat and boil the mixture to the hard-ball stage (121°C on a sugar thermometer), stirring to stop the cream in the mixture from scorching on the bottom of the saucepan. Take off the heat and stir in the vanilla essence. Immediately pour the syrup into the prepared cake tin.

When the caramel has started to firm up, use an oiled knife to mark it into squares or bars. When completely cold, turn the slab out of the tin, peel off the baking paper and use a sharp knife to cut the chewy caramel into neat pieces as marked.

Wrap the caramels individually in cellophane or waxed paper and store in an airtight container.

ROCKY ROAD BITES

MAKES 1 KG

150 g raisins

75 g dried cherries

80 ml orange liqueur, kirsch or fruit juice

150 g dark chocolate, roughly chopped

150 g milk chocolate, roughly chopped

150 g unsalted butter

1 tablespoon golden syrup

225 g shortcake or digestive biscuits,
roughly crushed

100 g chopped or mini marshmallows

Base-line a shallow, 20-cm square cake tin with baking paper.

Place the raisins and cherries in a bowl with the liqueur or juice. Stir, cover and leave to soak for several hours or overnight. Drain and reserve.

Place both types of chocolate in a large bowl with the butter and golden syrup. Place the bowl over a saucepan of simmering water and melt, stirring until smooth. Take off the heat and add the soaked fruit, biscuit pieces and marshmallows. Fold together until everything is well coated. Turn the mixture into the prepared cake tin and spread evenly. Cover and chill until hard.

Remove the rocky road from its tin and peel off the baking paper. Cut the slab into generous teatime pieces or dainty after-dinner bites to nibble on with coffee.

MINI FLORENTINES

A florentine is a pastry, most likely of French origin, that is a crunchy mix of nuts, candied cherries mixed with sugar, butter and honey. To add further decadence, the bottom is coated in chocolate.

MAKES 30

60 g unsalted butter
80 ml double cream
100 g caster sugar
100 g flaked almonds
100 g chopped almonds
100 g glacé cherries, chopped
50 g candied orange peel, finely chopped
grated zest of 1 orange
50 g plain flour
225 g dark chocolate

Preheat the oven to 180°C. Line two large baking sheets with baking paper.

Place the butter, cream and sugar in a heavy-based saucepan and heat, stirring, until the sugar dissolves. Bring to the boil, take off the heat, and stir in the almonds, cherries, candied peel, orange zest and flour.

Place small spoonfuls of the mixture well apart on the prepared baking sheets. Flatten each blob with a wet knife. Bake for 12 to 15 minutes, until they are golden and beginning to brown at the edges. Transfer to a wire rack to cool and crisp up.

Melt the chocolate in a bowl over a saucepan of simmering water. Spread one side of each florentine with chocolate and, as it begins to cool and firm, use a fork to comb the traditional pattern of wavy lines into the chocolate. When the chocolate has set completely, store the florentines in an airtight container.

Preserving and pickling were a normal part of life for our grandmothers' generation, and it's high time we brought back these clever and simple methods. These recipes are not only perfect for using up and preserving a glut of fruit and vegetables in the summer or autumn, but also they provide us with the delicious taste of strawberries or pickles all year.

Traditional Strawberry Jam

Blackberry and Apple Jelly

Citrus Marmalade

Zesty Lemon Curd

Summer Vegetable Ketchup

Essential Lemon Oil

Herbal Vinegar

Apple Sauce

Spiced Winter Pickle

Cranberry and Pear Chutney

Green Tomato Chutney
with Cumin

Rhubarb and Tomato Chutney

Sage and Garlic Jelly

PRESERVES,
PICKLES &
SAUCES

TRADITIONAL STRAWBERRY JAM

Our grandmothers and the women before them often made their own jam for family and friends. It is a great way to use up a seasonal glut of strawberries or other fruit from the garden, or with cheap boxes from the local market. Home-made jam on warm buttered toast is one of life's simple pleasures.

MAKES 6 X 250 G JARS

1.5 kg strawberries, hulled and halved
juice of 2 lemons
1.25 kg jam sugar

Place the strawberries and lemon juice in a saucepan and simmer very gently for 1 hour.

Add the sugar and turn up the heat until the mixture sets (105°C on a sugar thermometer). Skim any scum off the surface, then set aside until a skin starts to form. Pour into sterilized jars, seal them and leave to cool. Label and date the jars and store in a cool place. Can be kept for at least six months and store in the refrigerator once opened.

BLACKBERRY AND APPLE JELLY

The blackberries give this jelly a stunning deep-purple colour. The jelly is absolutely delicious with cheese and biscuits, particularly blue, Camembert or goats' cheese.

MAKES 4 X 250 G JARS
450 ml water
1.3 kg blackberries, washed
2 large cooking apples, peeled, cored and chopped
juice of 2 lemons
jam sugar (see method)

Bring 150 ml of cold water to the boil in a large saucepan, add the blackberries, apple pieces and lemon juice, and simmer for 20 minutes until the fruit is soft.

Transfer the fruit and juice to a sterilized jelly bag suspended over a large bowl and leave it to drip overnight. A colander lined with clean muslin can also be used. Be patient and don't be tempted to squeeze the bag because this will make the jelly cloudy.

Measure the juice in a jug and then return it to a preserving pan or very large saucepan. For every 600 ml of juice add 450 g of sugar. Bring to the boil and simmer for up to 15 minutes, spooning away any bubbly residue that forms.

To test for setting, chill a small plate. Put a spoonful of the hot jelly mixture onto the plate and place in the refrigerator for 5 minutes. Now push the edge of the jelly with your finger – if it wrinkles, setting point has been reached.

Carefully pour the hot liquid into sterilized jars, seal and store in a cool, dark place.

CITRUS MARMALADE

MAKES ABOUT 2 KG

2 oranges, halved
2 lemons, halved
1 grapefruit, halved
2 kg granulated sugar

Set a cloth-lined sieve over a bowl. Ideally using a wooden reamer, juice the fruit over the sieve, scouring the shells and leaving the pips and membranes caught in the cloth. Reserve the juice.

Tie the cloth into a loose bag and put it in a pan with 2 litres of cold water. Slice the skins finely, add them to the pan and leave to soak overnight.

The next day, bring to the boil, then simmer until the peel is meltingly tender. Remove the bag, squeeze its juices back into the pan and discard the residue. Add the sugar and the reserved juice. Heat gently, stirring until the sugar has dissolved completely. Raise the heat and boil hard to setting point – when a spoonful of the liquid dropped onto a chilled plate thickens enough to wrinkle when you push a finger through it.

Remove from the heat and let the marmalade cool for about 10 minutes before ladling it into warm, sterilized jars. Cover until cold before sealing the tops. Store in a cool, dark place.

ZESTY LEMON CURD

Lemon curd is one of those really handy pantry staples that can be used in so many ways. It can be added to eclairs, cakes, biscuits and tarts. It is also delicious on hot, buttered toast.

MAKES 3 X 250 G JARS
225 g unsalted butter, melted
450 g caster sugar
3 tablespoons grated lemon zest
150 ml lemon juice
pinch of salt
4 eggs, beaten until frothy

Pour the melted butter into a heatproof bowl and add the sugar, lemon zest and juice, and the salt. Stir until the sugar has dissolved.

In a separate bowl, stir a good spoonful of the lemon mixture into the beaten eggs. Pour the egg mixture into the remaining lemon mixture and place the bowl over a pan of simmering water to cook for 7 to 10 minutes until thick. Ladle into sterilized jars, cover and leave to cool.

Store in the refrigerator.

SUMMER VEGETABLE KETCHUP

Home-made ketchup is such a treat. This recipe includes garlic, herbs and spices, which give the sauce a savoury complexity that is delicious with so many dishes.

MAKES 1 LITRE

60 ml olive oil
2 onions, finely chopped
2 celery sticks, trimmed and finely chopped
3 carrots, trimmed and finely chopped
3 garlic cloves, crushed
sprig of sage, leaves stripped
sprig of rosemary, leaves stripped
1 bay leaf
1.5 kg ripe tomatoes, skinned
70 g brown sugar
125 ml red wine vinegar
1 teaspoon salt
1 teaspoon cayenne pepper

Heat the olive oil in a large saucepan and gently fry the onions, celery and carrots until soft. Add the garlic, fresh herbs and bay leaf, and cook for a further minute or two. Remove the bay leaf and put the mixture into a food processor. Blend until smooth, then return to the saucepan.

Place half the skinned tomatoes in the food processor and process until smooth. Add to the saucepan with the rest of the tomatoes and the remaining ingredients. Bring the mixture to the boil and then simmer, covered, for 30 minutes. Pour into sterilized jars, seal and use within three months.

ESSENTIAL LEMON OIL

MAKES 225 ML

grated zest of 2 unwaxed lemons
225 ml olive oil

Place the lemon zest and oil in a small saucepan and warm gently for 3 minutes. Remove from the heat and leave to cool. Transfer to a bowl, cover and infuse for 24 hours.

Strain the oil into a sterilized bottle and store in the refrigerator for up to one month.

HERBAL VINEGAR

MAKES 1 BOTTLE

fresh herbs of your choice: basil, lemon balm, rosemary, mint, oregano and bay leaves are all good
sufficient white wine vinegar or cider vinegar to fill your chosen bottle(s)

Wash and dry the fresh herbs gently and pack them into a sterilized jar. Fill the jar with vinegar, seal and store in a dark place at room temperature. Leave for three to six weeks, depending on how strong you want the taste to be. Strain the vinegar through a muslin cloth and transfer to a freshly sterilized bottle. Add one or two fresh sprigs of one of your chosen herbs before sealing.

APPLE SAUCE

Sweet and slightly spicy, this is the perfect accompaniment to roast pork and crackling. Alternatively, this simple recipe can be used as filling for individual apple pies.

SERVES 6 TO 8

500 g cooking apples, chopped
grated zest of 1 lemon
2 tablespoons caster sugar
1 cinnamon stick
60 ml water
60 g unsalted butter
pinch of salt

Place all the ingredients in a saucepan, cover and cook over a low heat for about 10 minutes until the apples are soft and mushy.

Remove the saucepan from the heat and discard the cinnamon stick before serving. The sauce can be kept in the refrigerator for one week or in the freezer for up to a year.

SPICED WINTER PICKLE

MAKES 500 G

1 large cauliflower, trimmed
  and broken into florets
3 onions, diced
3 carrots, peeled and sliced
1 cucumber, peeled, deseeded and sliced
1 red pepper, deseeded and sliced
  into fine strips
200 g fine green beans, trimmed and
  chopped into 2.5-cm pieces
100 g salt
70 g plain flour
2 teaspoons curry powder
2 teaspoons ground turmeric
2 teaspoons mustard powder
2 teaspoons ground ginger
1 litre white wine vinegar
150 g granulated sugar

Place all the prepared vegetables into a large mixing bowl and toss with the salt. Transfer to a colander, cover and leave in the kitchen sink for 12 hours or overnight.

Wash the salted vegetables in several changes of water and return them to the colander to drain thoroughly.

Place the flour and spices into a very large saucepan or preserving pan and heat gently, stirring constantly. Gradually pour in the vinegar, stirring all the time to make sure no lumps form. Stir in the sugar and bring to the boil – the mixture should thicken. Add the prepared vegetables to the saucepan, stir well to combine with the spicy sauce and cook for a further 3 minutes until all the vegetables are hot.

Pour into sterilized jars and seal immediately. Store for four weeks before using.

CRANBERRY AND PEAR CHUTNEY

MAKES 3 X 250 G JARS

1 small onion, finely chopped
1 pear, cored and finely chopped
1 tablespoon red wine vinegar
1 tablespoon brandy
225 g fresh or frozen cranberries
55 g brown sugar
½ teaspoon mixed spice
½ teaspoon ground cinnamon
½ teaspoon ground ginger

Place the onion, pear, vinegar and brandy in a large saucepan and cook gently for 10 minutes until the onion and pear have softened.

Stir in the cranberries, sugar and spices, and cook for a further 15 minutes or so until the cranberries split and the liquid is reduced to a thick consistency.

Leave to cool, then store in a steralized jar in the refrigerator for up to two weeks.

GREEN TOMATO CHUTNEY WITH CUMIN

MAKES 6 X 250 G JARS

1.3 kg small green tomatoes, skinned
and chopped
700 ml white wine vinegar
900 g caster sugar
½ teaspoon ground cumin

Place the tomatoes in a large saucepan with the vinegar, sugar and cumin, and boil rapidly for 5 minutes. To preserve the chutney, transfer it while still hot to sterilized jars and seal immediately. The seal will tighten as the chutney cools. Alternatively, the chutney can be stored in jars or covered bowl in the refrigerator for one week.

RHUBARB AND TOMATO CHUTNEY

MAKES 800 G

45 ml honey
500 g rhubarb, washed, peeled and chopped
into 2-cm chunks
400 g tomatoes, skinned and chopped
1 tablespoon vinegar
1 pinch cinnamon
1 chilli
1 pinch curry powder
1 pinch ginger
1 pinch salt

Heat the honey in a saucepan, add the rhubarb and swirl around to cover. Leave to soften slowly for 5 minutes over a low heat. Add the remaining ingredients to the pan, mix well and cook for a further 5 minutes, slowly. Remove the pan from the heat and pour the chutney straight into sterilized jars. Leave to cool at room temperature before storing in the fridge.

SAGE AND GARLIC JELLY

MAKES APPROXIMATELY 1.4 KG

900 g cooking apples, chopped
large bunch of sage, plus 3 or 4 sprigs
1 head of garlic, halved, plus 2 cloves,
  peeled and finely sliced
250 ml cider vinegar
1 teaspoon salt
approximately 1.2 kg granulated sugar

Place the chopped apples in a large saucepan. Add the bunched sage, bruised, and the whole head of garlic. Pour in the vinegar, add the salt and enough cold water to cover. Bring to the boil. Simmer, partially covered, until the apple is very soft. Strain through a clean cloth, letting the liquid drip into a bowl overnight.

Measure the juice and return it to the saucepan. Add 225 g of sugar for every 300 ml of juice. Heat, stirring, until the sugar has dissolved completely. Add the finely sliced garlic to the saucepan. Boil rapidly to setting point – when a spoonful of the liquid dropped onto a chilled plate wrinkles when you push a finger through it. Remove from the heat and cool for about 10 minutes. Add a sprig of blanched sage to each warm, sterilized jar before filling with jelly. Cover until cold before sealing with vinegar-proof lids.

INDEX

BAKER'S NOTES

INGREDIENTS

BUTTER: Depending on what you are making, the temperature of the butter can play an important role. For cakes, bring the butter up to room temperature; for pastry use chilled, cubed butter.

EGGS: When whipping eggs for cake batters it is best to bring them to room temperature first.

BAKING POWDER: Baking powder lasts a long time but not forever. To check it is still good to use, drop a spoonful into hot water and if it fizzes it is still active and good to use.

SAFETY NOTES

When preserving, pickling and making sauces it is essential to steralize the jars before filling as this keeps your creations fresh and guards against potentially harmful bacteria.

OVEN TEMPERATURES

WITHOUT FAN	FAN		
140°C	120°C	(275°F)	Gas Mark 1
150°C	130°C	(300°F)	Gas Mark 2
160°C	140°C	(325°F)	Gas Mark 3
180°C	160°C	(350°F)	Gas Mark 4
190°C	170°C	(375°F)	Gas Mark 5
200°C	180°C	(400°F)	Gas Mark 6
220°C	200°C	(425°F)	Gas Mark 7
230°C	210°C	(450°F)	Gas Mark 8
240°C	220°C	(475°F)	Gas Mark 9